XTREME FISH

Catfish

BY S.L. HAMILTON

A&D Xtreme
An imprint of Abdo Publishing | www.abdopublishing.com

Visit us at
www.abdopublishing.com

Published by Abdo Publishing Company, a division of ABDO, PO Box 398166, Minneapolis, Minnesota 55439. Copyright ©2015 by Abdo Consulting Group, Inc. International copyrights reserved in all countries. No part of this book may be reproduced in any form without written permission from the publisher. A&D Xtreme™ is a trademark and logo of Abdo Publishing Company.

Printed in the United States of America, North Mankato, Minnesota.
052014
092014

PRINTED ON RECYCLED PAPER

Editor: John Hamilton
Graphic Design: Sue Hamilton
Cover Design: Sue Hamilton
Cover Photo: Getty Images
Interior Photos: Alamy-pgs 18-19; AP-pgs 7 (top), 8, 9 & 29 (top & bottom); Dreamstime-pgs 12-13 & 16-17; Getty Images-pgs 6, 7 (bottom), 14-15, 19 (inset), 20-21, 24-25 & 26-27; Glow Images-pgs 22-23; RavenFire Media-illustrations pgs 20 & 24; Thinkstock-pgs 1, 2-3, 4-5, 10-11, 28, 30-31 & 32.

Websites
To learn more about Xtreme Fish, visit booklinks.abdopublishing.com. These links are routinely monitored and updated to provide the most current information available.

Library of Congress Control Number: 2014932240

Cataloging-in-Publication Data

Hamilton, S. L.
 Catfish / S. L. Hamilton.
   p. cm. -- (Xtreme fish)
Includes index.
ISBN 978-1-62403-447-3
1. Catfishes--Juvenile literature.   2. Marine animals--Juvenile literature.   I. Title.
597/.49--dc23

2014932240

Contents

Catfish

Catfish are easily recognized by their distinctive "barbels," which look like a cat's whiskers. Different species are found in both freshwater and saltwater around the world.

Some catfish grow to enormous sizes, as much as 650 pounds (295 kg) or more! They do not have big teeth, but are armed with pointed quills in their fins, making them a dangerous catch.

XTREME FACT – The Mekong, wels, and goonch catfish species grow monstrously big. They have been known to swallow and drown humans.

Species & Location

There are more than 3,500 species of catfish. They have existed for about 80 million years. Catfish are found in and around every continent except Antarctica.

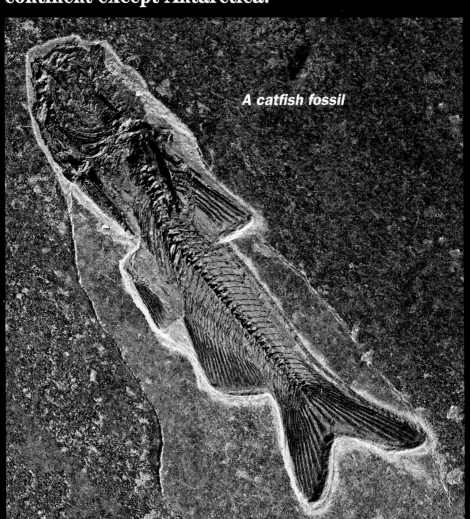

A catfish fossil

A catfish rests at the bottom of a river.

Catfish can live in many different habitats. Typically, they prefer to reside at the bottom of rivers or lakes. There are even air-breathing catfish. Walking catfish move using their sharp-quilled fins. As long as they stay damp, they do not need to be in the water.

Walking Catfish

XTREME FACT– One in every five fish on Earth is a species of catfish.

Size

Typical catfish found in North America include channel catfish, blue catfish, bullhead, madtom, and stonecat. These fish are usually 2 to 5 pounds (.9 to 2.3 kg), but can grow much bigger. The largest North American blue catfish caught was 130 pounds (59 kg).

Kansas anglers hold an 82-pound (37-kg) blue catfish caught in April 2013. The fish broke size records for the state.

Europe, Russia, and Asia have human-sized catfish. These monster fish may weigh hundreds of pounds and measure more than 10 feet (3 m).

Anglers near Barcelona, Spain, haul in a huge catfish in 2005. The fish was 7'7" (2.3 m) long and weighed 212 pounds (96 kg). The anglers later released the catfish back into the water.

Shape

Although different species of catfish are shaped differently, most have heavy, flat heads with mouths at the bottom. Their weighty heads and small gas bladders make them "negatively buoyant." This means they sink. But these fish want to be at the bottom anyway. They use their flat heads to shovel through the mud to find food.

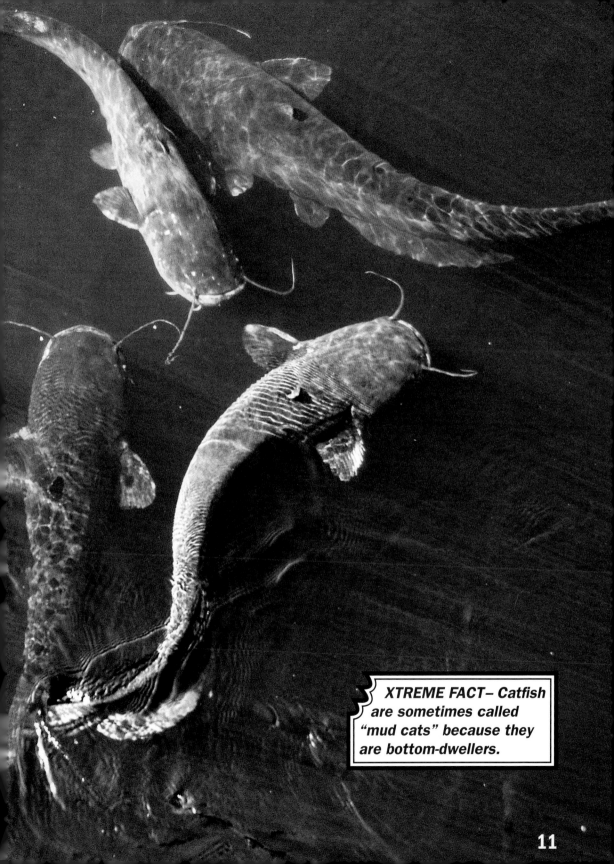

XTREME FACT– Catfish are sometimes called "mud cats" because they are bottom-dwellers.

Teeth & Mouth

Catfish have small teeth. They do not use them for biting their food. They have large mouths that suck in their prey.

A *close-up view of a channel catfish's mouth and teeth.*

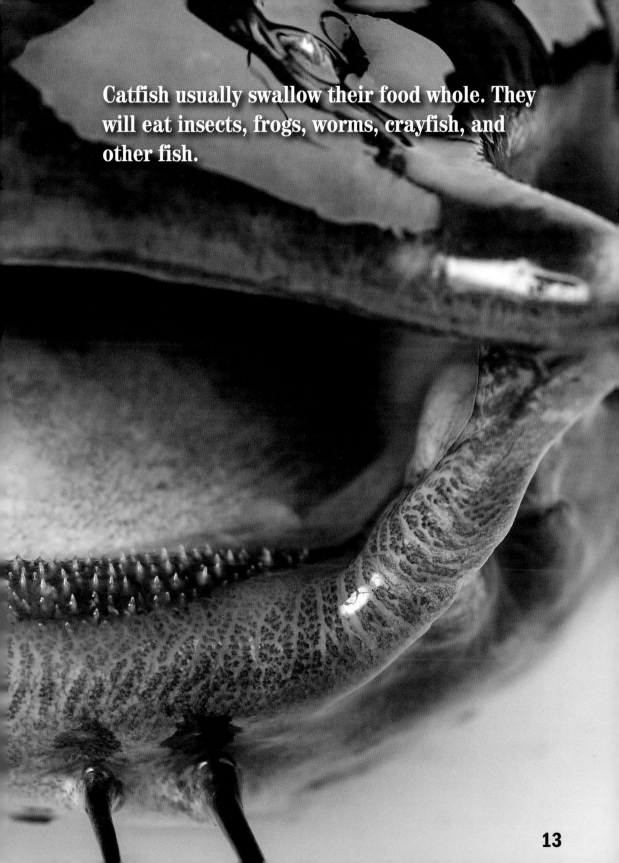

Catfish usually swallow their food whole. They will eat insects, frogs, worms, crayfish, and other fish.

Barbels

Whisker-like barbels are used to find food and help catfish feel their way through murky water. Catfish may have up to four pairs of barbels. They are located by the nose, on either side of the mouth, and on the chin. Some species have fewer sets.

The barbels contain most of a catfish's taste buds. The taste buds help the fish decide whether it wants to eat something or not. Catfish have more than 100,000 taste buds all over their bodies. Humans have about 10,000 on their tongues.

XTREME QUOTE –
"Catfish are swimming tongues. You can't touch any place on a catfish without touching thousands of taste buds."
–Dr. John Caprio, Louisiana State University

Sense of Smell

Although catfish use their barbels to help them find food, they also have a good sense of smell. There are olfactory (smell) organs in front of their eyes. They take in water and scents over tissue folds. The more folds, the better it can detect a scent. A channel catfish may have more than 140 folds, while a rainbow trout has only 18. A catfish's excellent sense of smell helps it find food.

Eyesight

Because catfish have other senses to help them find food and detect danger, they have small eyes. However, they still have good vision.

Catfish can see colors. They can see during the day and at night. Catfish watch for predators above and surrounding them. If they see the shadow of a bird, they will stay hidden and safe.

XTREME FACT– There are cave catfish that are blind. The Mexican blindcat lives in underground water in Mexico. It finds food using its barbels and other sensing organs.

Hearing

Catfish do not have ears, but they do have sensitive hearing. Sound waves, such as movements made by fish prey, travel through water and hit a catfish's body. The vibrations move to the fish's swim bladder. It starts vibrating.

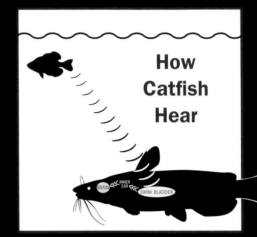

How Catfish Hear

BRAIN INNER EAR SWIM BLADDER

The swim bladder is connected by a series of bones to the catfish's inner ear. The sound message is then carried to the catfish's brain.

Lateral Line

Catfish also hear through a body part called the lateral line. This is a series of pores along the fish's side. Catfish detect surrounding vibrations, such as crayfish walking across the mud or fish jumping at the surface. Inside the pores, hairlike projections signal a catfish's brain when it "hears" movement.

Lateral Line

XTREME QUOTE – *"The Chinese have used catfish for centuries to warn of earthquakes. Catfish can detect days in advance a lot of earthquakes because they have an ultra-sensitivity to low frequency vibrations."*
–Dr. John Caprio, Louisiana State University

Electroreception

Living creatures give off electrical pulses. These electrical fields can be "felt" by certain creatures.

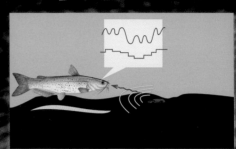

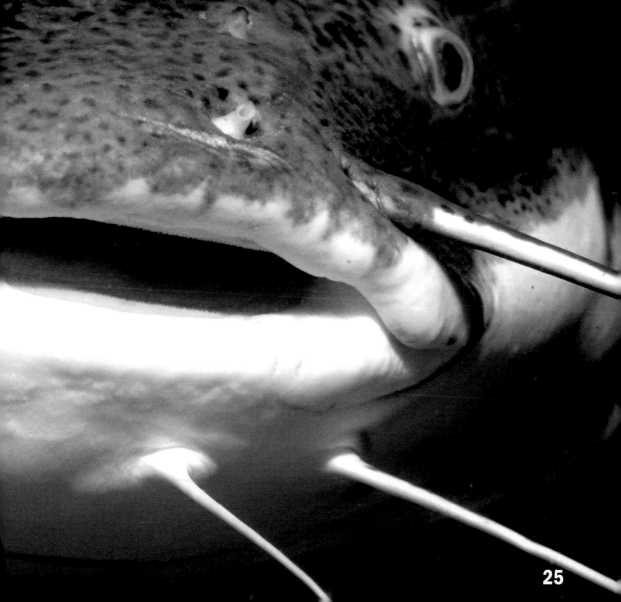

Sharks have electroreception. So do catfish. Special cells on a catfish's head and lateral line detect the presence of prey. If the catfish is within inches of its prey, it does not need to see or hear it. The catfish can dig through mud and find its dinner just by electric sense alone.

Attacks on Humans

Catfish may not have teeth, but they can protect themselves. They have strong, needle-like rays on their dorsal and pectoral fins that can lock in an upright position. These spines can inflict severe wounds.

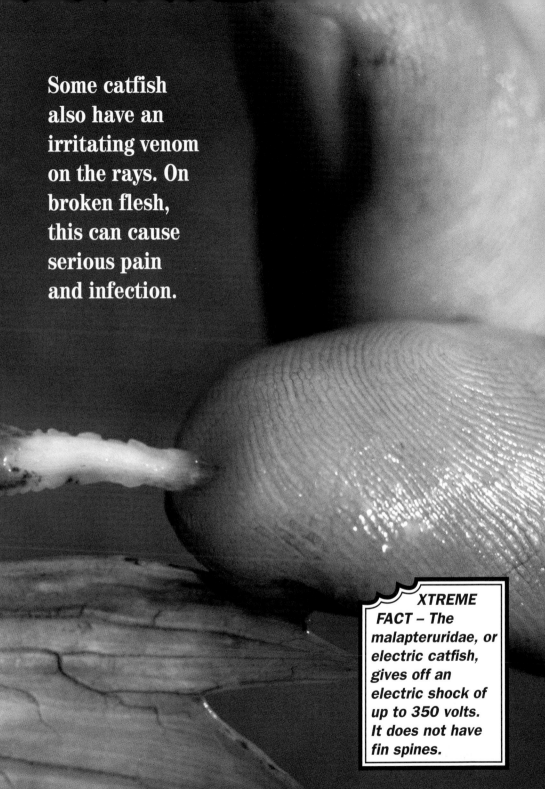

Some catfish
also have an
irritating venom
on the rays. On
broken flesh,
this can cause
serious pain
and infection.

XTREME
FACT – The
malapteruridae, or
electric catfish,
gives off an
electric shock of
up to 350 volts.
It does not have
fin spines.

Fishing for Catfish

Anglers around the world go after catfish. People eat them. There are even catfish farms. Hook-and-line fishing is used by many fishermen. Although most catfish average four to five pounds (1.8 to 2.3 kg), everyone wants to hook a monster "cat." Catfish can be caught day or night, but many anglers go in the evening, when catfish are less likely to see them.

Some catfish are so big, the only way to land them is to drag them to shore.

In 2005, a 646-pound (293-kg) Mekong giant catfish was caught in Thailand. It is believed to have been the world's heaviest living freshwater fish.

Noodling or grabbling is a type of fishing in which a person dives underwater and sticks their hand into a hole where a catfish may be. When the catfish swallows the hand or arm, the person then pulls the catfish up.

Noodling is illegal in parts of the United States. People may drown or be attacked by other predators, such as alligators or snapping turtles.

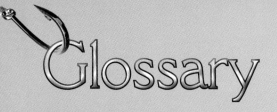

Glossary

BARBELS
Whisker-like organs found near the mouths of certain fish such as catfish. The barbels act as taste buds.

BUOYANT
Allowing something to float in the surrounding air or water in which it lives. Catfish are "negatively buoyant," meaning they sink to the bottom of the water in which they live, where they are safer, and where they find food.

DORSAL FIN
The fin that is located on the top of a fish's back. On a shark, for example, the dorsal fin is the one that sticks out of the water when the shark is swimming near the surface.

LATERAL LINE
A visible line that runs along the sides of fish. The lateral line helps fish detect movement in the water. The sensing organ helps fish to find prey and helps them avoid becoming prey.

MEKONG GIANT CATFISH
The world's largest freshwater fish, found in the Mekong River in Southeast Asia. This catfish is distinctive because it has nearly no barbels on its face. It is a threatened species.

OLFACTORY
Olfactory refers to the sense of smell.

PECTORAL FIN
Fins found behind a fish's head, on either side of its body.

QUILL / RAY
A sharp, bone-like spine inside some fish's fins. Often used to defend themselves. Walking catfish move on dry land using the strong rays in their fins.

SWIM BLADDER
A sac inside the body of a fish that holds gas. It is also known as a gas bladder or air bladder. It helps a fish adjust buoyancy and move to different water depths.

TASTE BUDS
Organs that identify edible items. In a human, taste buds are on the tongue. A catfish has taste buds all over its body.

VENOM
A poisonous liquid that may be used for killing or immobilizing prey, and for defense.

Index